How to Meditate Handbook

How to Meditate Handbook

For Beginners as well as experienced Meditators

Mansour Elkofairi

Published by Tablo

INTRODUCTION

A guide to meditation for beginners, experienced meditators and Spiritual seekers. Step by step instructions for those learning the fundamentals of meditation as well as techniques for achieving Stillness and altered states of consciousness.

*"**Stillness**", a level of separation, a place of "**Non Thought**"*

*Everything is 'Energy', all things in our world, our Universe are constantly in motion. Even objects that appear to be still are in fact vibrating, resonating at various frequencies. When you achieve Stillness it may feel as though "**Everything Stops Vibrating**", a peaceful calm state unlike anything you will experience in the physical.*

CHAPTER 1

STILLNESS

'The In-between State'

The aim of Meditation for many is achieving Stillness. Many people however meditate for years without ever really experiencing a level of Stillness, sad but true….allow me to explain.

Stillness is much more than a calm, quiet, motionless state. Yes you should sit quietly and calmly, yes you should be motionless! But stillness is an altered state of consciousness, a level of separation, a place of **"Non Thought"** you achieve from following a good meditative practice.

Everything is 'Energy', all things in our world, our Universe are constantly in motion. Even objects that appear to be still are in fact vibrating, resonating at various frequencies. When you achieve Stillness it will feel as though **"Everything Stops Vibrating"**, a peaceful calm state unlike anything you will experience in the physical.

The Dimensional Shift

Immediately before the shift into stillness you might feel a wave flow from the head downwards, a very real physical experience, a feeling of calmness (try not to be distracted by it), You will feel this inside the body as well as around the body. It is not a constant, and one shouldn't expect it every time, but on most occasions you will feel it, Its usually an indication you have made the dimensional shift into the in-between state.

I Made it! I'm There! What happens now?

That's entirely up to you….You choose what happens next, you are an Unlimited being. You may choose to enter the **Void** for a more spiritual experience, explore your subconscious, heal the physical and Spiritual body just to name a few, or simply sit in Stillness and appreciate the peace and quiet, reset your body and mind before or after a busy day.

How to Experience Stillness - the In-between State?

Keep it simple, develop a strong foundation, Discipline and daily practice. With so many different meditative practices available one can easily get lost and discouraged trying to find a technique or practice that suits their needs. Developing core meditation skills will establish a strong foundation. The following chapters we will cover

- Seating positions and Body Language (Chapter 2)
- 60 second Breathing technique and Body Relaxation (Chapter 3)
- Entering the 'All Knowing Mind' Secret technique (Chapter 4)
- Self Observation - (Chapter 5)
- Lets Meditate (Chapter 6)

CHAPTER 2

SEATING POSITIONS & BODY LANGUAGE

'Comfort above All'

Sit in a position that 'Works for You', i cant stress this enough. Your seating position should be comfortable with your Back Straight allowing your body to relax and muscles to drop without strain or tension. There are many meditative seating positions such as Full Lotus, Half Lotus, Burmese, Laying down or on a Chair to name a few. When learning to meditate i suggest sitting on a chair with feet flat on the ground back straight and hands cupped in your lap palms facing your abdomen, that helps to focus on the practice of meditation without worry about body position. When you become more confident then feel free to practice other seating or laying positions.(Note….please avoid stressful yoga seating positions when trying to meditate and NEVER sit with your legs crossed)

Laying Down *(not recommended for beginners)*

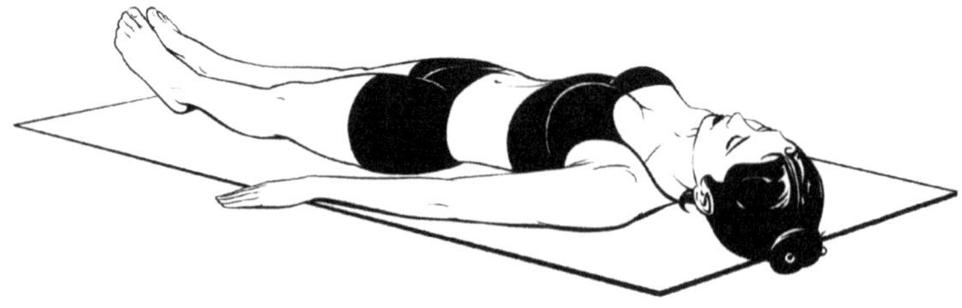

Meditation whilst laying down is very effective and can often lead to the most profound experiences, however....usually when laying down the body goes into sleep mode, and quite often you will fall asleep during the meditation. If you can manage to stay awake you will find it a quicker method to enter the void or the in-between state.

Comfort Level = 10/10

Sitting on a Chair *(recommended for beginners)*

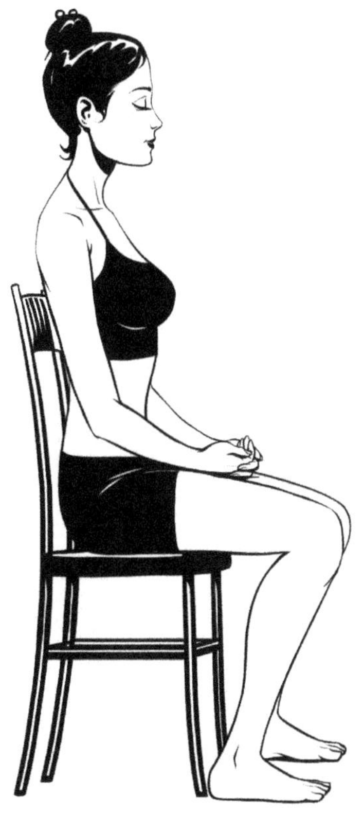

Sitting on a chair with back support is one of the best positions when learning how to meditate. In saying that many experienced meditators still use this seating position when practicing, also a good positon for anyone who suffers joint pains, back pain or arthritis. Remember to keep your legs at 90 degrees to the ground and feet flat on the floor.

Comfort Level = 8.5/10

Quarter Lotus *(recommended)*

In Quarter lotus, one leg is bent and resting on the ground, the other leg is bent with the foot resting on the opposite calf. The Quarter Lotus is one of the most common meditation seating positions and for good reason. This position allows your energy to focus in and closely around the body whilst supporting a straight back and good posture without overstressing the joints and ligaments in the knees.

Comfort Level = 8.5/10

Half Lotus *(recommended)*

In half lotus, one leg is bent and resting on the ground, the other leg is bent with the foot resting on the opposite thigh. Very Similar to the Half Lotus, offering the same in posture and support but with slightly less comfort.

Comfort Level = 7.5/10

Body Language

Hand placement is an important factor when meditating, again many practitioners will suggest multiple hand positions either on knees, palms facing down or upward, some suggest bringing certain fingers together whilst turning or placing the hands away from the body etc. None of which are recommended in this How to Meditate Handbook, the reason for this is due to the bodies energy and how energy flows in the direction it's given, normally the energy expands beyond the body, feeling it's surrounding area, try and imagine energy reaching out beyond your organic body like the tentacles of an octopus! something very similar is happening to each and everyone of us constantly with our energy field.

So when one stretches out their arms into various positions or places hands on knees you are in fact connecting with your surroundings whilst trying to meditate. This can be beneficial for those trying to meditate for Abundance, Energy work, Healing or simply trying to connect with the Natural environment, this practice however reduces the possibility of reaching an altered state of consciousness such as 'Non Thought' or 'Stillness' simply because you are too focused on holding your hands in an unfamiliar position for long periods of time.

Hand Placement

Hands placed in your lap, should be open and cupped, meaning one hand in the palm of the other, with palms facing the abdominal area of the body, the natural directional flow of energy through the hands is outward, when facing the body, energy is directed back into your body instead of away from the body, therefore directing your natural energy to circulate through and closely around you for a more centrally focused meditation as apposed to reaching out and around you feeling the environment you are in.

(Energy can be absorbed through the hands if one chose to practice energy work…however that is not a practice for a silent mind meditation).

Tip!… cup the dominant hand with the non-dominant, meaning the dominant hand is closest to the body, Why? I'm glad you asked, one of the distractions when shifting into an altered state of consciousness is relinquishing control or 'letting go'….this practice helps place the mind in a neutral state instead of one that is in constant control

CHAPTER 3

BREATHING TECHNIQUE AND BODY RELAXATION

Once seated in a comfortable position and just before the meditation begins is when the Breathing technique is applied. Its a very quick 60 second breathing exercise that should not be missed.

This breathing exercise will calm both your mind and body by up to 50% prior to commencing, making your meditation much more affective.

Begin by breathing in for 6 seconds….holding your breath for a further 6 seconds….then exhaling for 6 seconds, repeating the exercise 3 times before moving on. You will notice a calmness and deep relaxation, this is mainly due to the holding of the breath after each breath in. The relaxing feeling is due to the exhale, a sense of relief overcomes the body. (take notice of the subtle change within. become familiar with that feeling and in time you will be able to call upon this feeling at will).

The human brain is constantly thinking, constantly bringing ideas and thoughts forward to the conscious mind, when you hold your breath the brain shifts it's attention to circulating oxygen and less focus on thoughts.

is without saying it in your mind, the same applies with numbers, street signs etc, see the word (or number) know it without repeating it.

Let's practice…

With eyes closed, begin at the number 25…..see the number 25 in front of you, watch it drift away from you as the next number '24' takes it's place and repeat…counting down to zero without actually saying the words in your mind, just see them as your counting down. you will immediately feel a subtle shift in your awareness, a focus inward.

If you trip and accidently say the word that identifies the number that's ok, don't be angry with yourself, it will take some time to master, just continue with the count down

Practice….practice….practice makes perfect.

This technique also works well when preparing for Astral travel. It will not only help with meditation but sharpen your mental skills in everyday life as well as fine tune your Intuition.

CAUTION! practicing this technique can and will aid in the activation of mental abilities especially in awareness and identifying with the 'I', the true self.

CHAPTER 5

<u>SELF OBSERVATION</u>

Self Observation is an awareness exercise where you turn your attention inward, watching your thoughts, feelings and Emotions without interacting with those same thoughts and feelings, simply observing them from a third person point of view.

If you find it difficult to understand, try and imagine being at the Movies or Cinema, sitting quietly and watching events in the movie unfold without interacting with the characters of the movie, just watching, observing.

By observing yourself you are watching your own movie, but most importantly without 'judgement', the moment you begin to judge your thoughts or feelings you begin to follow or interact with your thoughts and slide back into the ego. The idea of self observation is to separate from the 'Ego' and by observing yourself and watching your thoughts pass through your mind will eventually allow you to experience 'Non Thought' or 'Separation from Ego'.

'A judgemental mind will never see the truth'

The most important thing to remember when observing yourself is 'Non Judgement', i cant stress this enough, if using this technique to work through troubling thoughts or memories from life experience you must learn to do it without judging your actions or other peoples actions, simply observe, then and only then will you see the truth of the thoughts or memories, you will see previous life problems unravel before you and fade away, you will feel a sense of relief from the centre of the brain, sometimes even a popping sound as the thought leaves you, no longer troubling you or causing you pain.

'Do Not Focus….Just observe '

Many meditation practitioners and instructors use the word 'Focus', unfortunately one can not achieve Non thought during meditation whilst being focused. When you focus on an object or yourself you are interacting with the brain and therefore not achieving 'Non Thought'. Simply observe using your awareness instead, staying in a neutral state of mind without thought or emotion.

'Observing The Breath'

We want to use this same exercise to observe the breath during meditation. Once the meditation begins shift your awareness to the breath. Simply watch the breath as it passes the back of the throat area on the inhale and the same on the exhale. This is easier said than done with so many thoughts produced by the brain each moment. Thoughts will rise and you will interact or follow the thought, try not to get frustrated with yourself, gently shift your awareness back to the breath. Be kind and gentle with yourself.

If you find it difficult to stay aware of the breath try this training tip until it becomes second nature -

Training Tip : Count each inhale and exhale until you reach the number 10, if you become distracted by a thought and loose your count begin again from the beginning...Breath in...breath out...1) Breath in...breath out 2) ...and so on.

This will help train the mind to stay aware of the breath.

Practice...Practice...Practice...makes perfect.

Step 2- Get comfortable

- Sit in your chosen seating position, one that is comfortable, without strain and assists with keeping your back straight.

Step 3- Breathing Technique

- Begin your breathing exercise - inhale for 6 seconds, hold for 6 seconds, exhale for 6 seconds….repeat 3 times.

Step 4- Body Relaxation Technique

- Relax your body as stated in chapter 2, remember… do not spend too much time or focus too strenuously on this part, it should be effortless and quick

Step 5- The Countdown

- Begin the countdown technique as stated in chapter 3, starting from 25 and counting down to 0, remember to see the numbers as your counting down without saying the numbers in the mind.

(by this stage you should have practiced this technique several times in preparation)

Step 6- Be Aware of the breath

- Now gently shift your awareness to the breath and keep it there for the duration of the session, observing the inhale and exhale as stated in chapter 4

You are Source Energy, you are God Force, You are Eternal Being.

Good luck my friend, I hope this information reaches you and serves you well....with love and gratitude I hope to see you on the other side....Happy Journeys

CPSIA information can be obtained
at www.ICGtesting.com
Printed in the USA
BVHW040546220921
617191BV00016B/1523